Hi Kim,

Enjoy the book

First edition sept 22/2021

Patrick Walsh

Poetic Philosophical Views through
a Science of Artful Poetic Communication

Viewpoints and Points to View

PATRICK WALSH

ISBN: 978-1-6671-1371-5 (sc)
ISBN: 978-1-6671-1370-8 (hc)
ISBN: 978-1-6671-1369-2 (e)

Library of Congress Control Number: 2021908376

Author photo by AZIZ LADHA Photography

Lulu Publishing Services rev. date: 05/05/2021

Quiet! Sound not, nor take.
Await! And hear
a motion, in no solid mass.
Am I able to view the unseen,
then to be aware of what isn't, to see
what is.
Quite. Awaken, and have now that wisdom of silence,
The true teacher and master of peace.

Patrick Walsh

Dedication

I am dedicating this book to My Love Grace. We were going to celebrate the book release, my birthday and a Formal Marriage in May 2021. I was caring for her 24/7 until I could no longer do it alone. After only a few weeks having been admitted to a long-term care facility, she passed away April 2021.

For all of you who suffered a similar fate in Gracie's Name let Grace and I dedicate this book to you as well. Some of the proceeds of the book will go to paying for a book to be given to the families of those who lost a love one to Covid-19 in Nursing Homes, Long-term care Facilities and Hospitals. Please send a book to anyone you know who has suffered the loss of their loved ones in these facilities or elsewhere. This I am doing in Grace's Memory.

The Name Grace is of Latin origin and was first used as a reference to the Phrase "God's Grace or The Grace of God". It is fitting therefore that I by the Grace of God, bestow upon you this gift of poetry in the Memory of My Love Companion, Grace.

Remembrance

We remember you, your smile and all what you had to say,
kind words through our troubled days.

We remember you and the truth you spoke, giving us your wisdom
to help us cope.

We remember you when we played, I was a child sliding down the
hill on a sleigh.

We remembered you at graduation, after all the years, you sup-
ported me, so I could grow up one day and succeed.

We remember you when you held me close, your touch, I loved
the most.

We remember the times that as difficult they maybe, you were
always there just for me.

We remember the songs we sang, and the prayers we spoke, to
believe in God with all our heart, to him we shall return, leaving
behind children to learn.

We remember too, things we should not say, speaking in hate towards others, especially not our sisters and brothers.

We remember the walks and talks that seemed to ease the pain, when life at times seemed so insane.

We remember too all what was promised to come, that one day we could stand in the sun and say, we won.

We remember the smell in the kitchen at each and every meal, knowing we were loved and love is what we could feel.

We remember when you taught me to ride and drive, teaching to respect other drivers, so we could get home safe and always on time, to wake in the morning to more sunshine.

There are so many memories and mentioned are just a few, in my thoughts of you. Who gave me life, one I can't repay? My prayers are now with you as you lay in your grave. Sand to cover the body while the soul departs. It seems my heart is falling apart. For all what you have given me, I can't seem to let go. Why couldn't you live, until you grew old? In passing am I to understand, that God has a better plan, than just being a Man.

A mystery, but I must believe, you are in a better place that I can't see. If it be your will, while I stand here now, to know you are not gone, and not far away, while your body is buried in the grave.

So, I shall live in your spirit as you speak, no longer do I need to weep. Angel present you are one, this day is over, this day is done.

Preface

Philosophy should be a reach and journey into the realm of the unknown, made known through a scientific process that allows for self-discovery of truths thought of, but not fully realized. That process to me as a poet and philosopher is looking at what is to be observed, to bring a certainty of it through the symbolism of words, so that through poetic language it can be communicated.

An artist's creativity requires a high level of awareness and ability. Such creativity lifts the progress of humanity's thinking upward, toward freedom of expression and thought.

Art can serve a higher purpose. For example, assisting in the manifestation of new realities that are desired by one and all.

Art is an enemy to those who want things to be kept always the same, without meaning and purpose. Art then, as a weapon, can pierce the hearts of those enemies like none other.

Use words, not bullets to make a change. Use music to mellow the heart.

Use dance to romance Mankind into poetic movements, to display the beauty we all hold within.

Then we have a chance to begin again.

Always exist in the moment, for in that moment is the creation of whatever is or will be. It is not limited by the past or the future, for you are responsible for what will become or end.

While isolated from the reality of our everyday existence, we need to give in services to others and bring to our souls a new meaning of presence. In the philosophical views we have through our poetry of thought, we communicate a purpose of a higher manifestation of reality, spiritual in nature, while being applicable in living.

In the presence of greatness, we endeavor to rise to an elevated state. The greatness we share is that we the human race carry with us the seed of a new horizon, where Mankind will be free to be, to be, to be. We are now to be no longer just man, to live and die without knowing why. We can know and know how to know the truth, that we are the science of our own thought. The mysteries of yesterday need not blind us from seeing tomorrow for how it should be. It is up to you to decide if you will rise or fall in the call to liberate all. We serve to give, to give how we serve, to save those to live another day.

Acknowledgments

I would like to give a special thanks to those who helped me in my life and contributed to my success in the production, and promoting of this book. Not all of them are named here.

First on the list would be my Creator.

Second would be my Parents who gave me life and the opportunity to go free.

Thirdly would be the heartbeat of love from my brothers and sisters God blessed me with.

A Special thanks, to My Golden-Haired Friend and His Friends that without their support my ability and potential to Survive to write now and serve others would not be possible.

Special thanks, to Prithvi for donating his time to produce films on my poetic writings.

A Special Thanks, to Natalie for her continued editing and consulting support.

Special thanks, to Sheryl and Tim for being such good friends.

A special thanks, to Jerry for his help.

A special thanks to Earl for teaching me communication and confront which was the single most important ability gained in my success in living.

A Special thanks to Aziz Ladha for his Photograph of me, editing and studio videography work.

I would like to thank Vincent Walsh for his consulting and editng work.

A special thanks to my friends from India for promoting my short films and book.

Our hearts are with you from Canada for the tragedies in people's lives due to Covid-19.

1

My Introduction of Self

Introducing oneself to others in the reality of truth is a challenging affair. When the events of one's life do not really reveal who one is or what one is doing, one finds oneself alone, without the understanding of those one loves most and those who should love one.

As the author of my own thoughts and life itself as I live it, it gives me a more truthful perspective. I am the only person who can truly speak to the reality of it. My communication will not be limited to the illusions or delusions of others as they see me, or even by the way I have been viewing myself and denying the integrity of my own reality of who I am.

I have chosen to awaken to my reality as a knowing being with the science of resolve within a subjective reality, conditionally limited to my existing physical identity. This awakening is coming into the enlightened state, where I see my physical form as a means to study experience for the benefit of self and others in service to the Supreme Being as one in our mutual causation of all life.

Being in an all-knowing state and achieving ultimate awareness removes us from reality, as we know it. Reality as we know it, however, has a basic purpose, and that is to study all life to survive in the present and, more importantly, to evolve toward the future.

Immortality is not a stable state without the technology of the source of knowledge that lies undiscovered within each of us.

The gradient scale of change for one and all requires experience to evolve to higher levels of ethics, ability, and potential.

My purpose in studying my life is to reveal truth to me for my own and others' benefit.

When you see me, do so through the words that I write, not through the blindness and ignorance of self or others. Those who see not the being I am seek only my demise and not the beauty and wealth I possess.

I come to you, then, as a being that cannot be fully seen or known through the perceptions of the body alone. It requires further enlightenment to perceive and be aware as a spirit to know me.

My introduction is then this: I am, so therefore I exist as me, a spirit, in the *I* of my own immortality, and came to be man among you to bring wisdom, love, friendship, and help through the words I speak. My desire is for you to enjoy my writing within the integrity of your own understanding of it.

Awake! Open.
The way is within.
To begin a journey.
Not of time.
But through your mind.

You're never alone.
To ride the wave.
To weather the storm.
And calm the day.

Dreaming is creating
from nothing.
Something you desire.
In life to admire.

I would if I could. But I won't if you don't.
And shouldn't if you
wouldn't.
Do the right thing.

Not knowing from within.
What you see has been.
To be what is not
and unable to start again.

I am who I am.
A spirit not a man.
Am I a man?
Why am I,
I, and a man?

Emptiness
is not providing within.
That which you are giving out
to be given again.
What was already
within.

Pain is failing
to find pleasure
through life's
stormy weather.

Friendless
is avoiding being
and seeing who you really are
and loving not that person
who you know to be unseen.

Who am I to this world
if what I am creating
is trampled to the ground
like an unwanted pearl?

Deciding to not
is restricting indeed
causing your heart
to forever bleed.

Dammed man
he sees not
those who kill his will

to give

to live

to have

to be glad.

Lost in lies
fried in earth's fuel
of torture
to be tomorrow's sorrow.

How can I let my soul
behold not the
beauty I have from
within and be not
what I could have been?

I am drifting away
as time passes by
into nowhere
without any reason why.

I have no feeling
no life to live
have no friend
no one to give me love
in a real way—
am I really in life's grave?

The fulfillment of knowledge
relies on the experience desired
to learn of the way
in how to remain in the game.

As life changes
so does the journey to consider
what that life is
without fear to face the unknown.

Quiet
unseen and without being heard
we act without regard
and are subject to lost realities
of what we could become, to
view who we are not,
and plot our own destruction.

We become deprived of life
when our souls will not in truth live
in the integrity of reason.

Our purpose is the guidepost to
what and where we should go
and what we should do
toward future thought and action
through our mental processes to win and avoid losses.

While looking you cannot see.
Within I am.
Yet you do not know.
Outside I exist
but you cannot find me.
From where do you perceive
to locate the spirit of who I am.

I am here
as I leave forever to be.

Are we blinded
by the ignorance of not knowing that we don't
and that we can't see
that we are blind
and imagine that we do?

Am I this thing
of a knowingness
consumed by my own knowingness
to know not that I am?

What blame would be needed
when responsibility is given to living
as we intended it to be
even if in an unknowing state?

Locked in a world of illusion
we isolate ourselves
behind walls of insecurities.

Is it not better to be weak
from the fear of the unknown
and through courage
face that fear by
confronting it
rather than to retreat
into a hiding place away from the true reality
of where we are?

Consumed by his unwillingness
to adventure into the world of the unknown
man becomes controlled by his fear within.

View change
to change the views and
master your own picture
of how you desire life to be.

When you view.
Do you look to see?
If what you see is what you see.
When you see
what you see.
And know that it is true.
Does it change?
Or remain the same, to be rational or insane?

Newness of life is looking at its illusions.
Agreed to be realities of existence.
Knowing you are creating it.
Being aware that this is so. And creating new ones
to have new illusions and realities.
Shared by agreements
to be aware of them to view.

Walking forgotten.
Who am I?
Have I left the self of who I am?
To who I am not to be.
In this reality of the forgotten me?

Sand bottom
without clay
molding through empty wind
to be blown away
to gather nowhere.

Life without
to shout not
or cry
why am I life without?

Knowing I know
and deciding I don't
won't free me but entrench who I am
into a state of depravity
that bounds me
into wounds of piercing untruths to believe
in the disbelief
that I know not what I know
and don't care to, is a lie of entrapment.

I want but can't have. I
have but I don't want.
What then am I to do
without what is?
If it is not desired to be or can't be had.

Maybe we have come from where
we never have been
to be in the place where
we once thought we were then.

I see the whisper
of the rainbow
hear my colors
when they flow.

Almost alive
but never to die
only to reach the beach of a new ocean
to ride a wave to freedom
from land and man
to soar again
I am the storm now of my own experience.

Never owning
only belonging to the life I serve
and deserve not what I take but
what I am given freely
for my pleasure from those I love.

Where I am
is not where you see me to be but far from the moment
that I began this journey to nowhere
to be somewhere far from here.

I long to be heard
and not ignored for the good I bring
and yet the music I sing
has no one to hear it
for in the melody is truth of what is here and now
that is not what was or should be.

Who will create a road for all to travel—
one made of spirit-paved marble
not of rocks
stones and gravel?

My heart weeps fulfilled not
walking closer
tortured by love sought.

Alone
I wait
but never to taste her beauty
to fulfill my need inside
to mend a broken heart
that needs to cry away what could not be
a love to have only in a dream.

Silent
and having no voice
because I choose not
to have a choice.

A man is as alive
and happy as he perceives and
can achieve those things in life
that he regards as worthwhile and aids in his survival.

In my experience of living
am I able to bring forward
my reality to experience it
or am I limited by thought
action and words to communicate that reality.

Create what you desire
and gain for others
what they admire
of what they see deep within of how to create and truly win.

Integrity is being your group
and your group being you
to have the power to do
what you want to.

If by chance you feel you will fail then
take some time to lose that tale for
the story that was told
is to prevent your success so loss will unfold
to keep you from doing your best.

Our integrity is our word
to establish a trust
to always do what we know we must
so what we say will always be true
for you to believe in me
and I in you.

Know yourself in life to explore
and you will never need to open or close a door
and in your heart you will know what is true
that true friends will always
be there for you.

You're never alone
to ride the wave
to weather the storm
and calm the day.

My moment in creation
taken from its appreciation
for not what it is
but what it is thought to be.

Dreams buried beneath
all what could not be
forced into slavery of mind of
things that cannot become or
be seen.

Crushed into a mass meaning
of yesterday's pain
of all life's weary moments
of why we came
to discover not but to rot away
from being anything imagined.

I am forever in the sky
and where I go
I don't know why but
when I get there
I will see and then when the sun goes down
I will be with me.

I have no feeling
no life to live
have no friend
no one to give me love in a real way
am I really in life's grave?

At the beginning he sat
at where he was
to discover he was not where he should be
he moved to now sit again
and found where he was then at the time he began.

Quiet

sound not nor take

await

and hear a motion in no solid mass

am I able to view the unseen then

to be aware of what isn't

to see what is

quiet awaken

and have now that wisdom of silence

the true teacher and master of peace.

I am listening
feeling your words of thought
absorbing not any unwanted sound
only the truth that you speak
with my soul
will I have what you say letting it settle as you weep.

Come walk with me
Let me take your hand
Come walk with me
I am more than a man
I can see your way and feel your pain
Come walk with me there is no shame
No sorrow inside
Come walk with me and fly away
Fly away for life is in and of you
Come walk with me
and know the truth.

We'll smile at the day
as it passes us by
knowing in our hearts
this love will never die.

Give our life the moment
that makes our dreams come true
we will always be together
me and you
even when we are down and no one else will care
we will be for each other always near.

Where are you
to be in your will
for truth that only you
can bring to a table of joy

Anew!
Rise from the graveyard of uncertainty
to exist of this desert land of broken man
And leave the heart of yesterday
laid deep within
To keep you out
of what is to be in freedom's wind
To blow you free away
into the unknown.

Lifeless
empty of feeling
passing out of time
to be against the wind of hopeless moments
that take away what could be
before a blossom of beauty
is created to please our inner sight that only a soul can view
Leaving an empty shell of our creation in a hollow hall of forgotten souls.

When I speak
unseen are the words of my creations
for within are moments
of truths unknown.

Listen for I hear a sound
unheard of
to lend that music of who I am
as cause of man
and his purpose to behold all wisdom of the how and why of existence
to capture in brief the reason
you and I are here.

Let my thoughts caress the minds of wanting souls
to fulfill their desire for me.
A thirst for knowledge that what can be is in the desire to become.

If you feel you lost
then at what cost
to learn and win
or to never try again.

Plan for your future
and see it through
there is always new things
that you can do.

Send me your thoughts
of who you are
and who I am not
for me to become the person
that I am
a much better man.

Sometimes I wonder
what this life will bring
Will it be a future or the past
where only a shadow is cast
of what could have been?

What about in time
if it does not seem to work will I keep trying
or will I desert my purpose
that is deep within
to keep going until I win?

If my friend tells me what to do
will I listen if what is said is true
Or will I go on my own way
and wished that where I came from
that I had stayed
And used what was said to continue to try
Instead of being alone and wondering why.

I am not succeeding
while others do
the answer my friend
lies within you.

Regard communication as the only route
to true happiness.

Develop a mind
that serves the spirit
of who you are.

Refuse to allow your mind
to be a tool
to enslave your soul and body in life.

Simple truths
are without confusion
to keep us from living
in a delusion.

Seek to believe not and
be without the insight
into your reality of what is
and be enslaved by the lies
that you have decided to become.

Never assume
that you have all the answers
but explore the unknown
to learn from what is known about what isn't.

Never place yourself beneath anyone
but respect your own self-worth
and that of others
and help humankind be the best he can be
instead of condemning him
for the worst that he has become.

Promise me a way
and lend me a hand
so I can lift myself out of this
desert land of man.

When lonely hearts forget what it was
they see not now what could be
and leave the present
to never see the beauty
of their creations.

Like a captured prey
we scream to be free
from the trap of our own illusions
of false realities.

Let me not be guided
by the inflamed meaning of gossip-mongering persons
who through selfish means
attempt to degrade the spirit of others and in envy they seek to destroy.

May we bring
our hearts divine
to all who come
with troubled minds.

May we lift up in
how we instruct
and not to offend
with our conduct.

May we give
and not take and fail
to relate to a needy soul
before it is too late.

In a cave where the walls around
are the barriers of the soul the
darkness of unknowing
knowingness of truths never told.

Moving through space and time
of reality that seems to have no end
In it lays traps of pleasures
to fulfill our desires
and meaning for men.

Our integrity
is our word to establish a trust
to always do
what we know we must.

If in making a mistake
you don't know why
you will never learn
if you don't give another try.

Know your life and what it is for
then you will never need to open or close a door
For in your heart you will know it is true
that how you are living is for you.

Somewhere inside
you will find a way
so that another person too can say
I too have trust within
that I have the strength to begin again.

Lifetime after lifetime
pained by hatred
from those who enslave
buried in earth's grave.

The difference between
what a man believes
and one who knows
is the certainty of his integrity of truth.

If you are always trying
to be understood
what will you ever come to understand?

Forgiveness
is having the strength to experience
what may be unforgivable
and the willingness to love anyway

Am I to be then
what I am now
and what I have been
to be again and again
yet I am the same?

Who are we
in this life of mystery
to live without certainty?

Be as you are
and you will always become
who you were to be.

The idea of infinity
is to be somewhere
from the viewpoint you are nowhere
to arrive in infinity somewhere.

The illusion of distance
from beginning to an end to view
gives us a space
to occupy.

Time you are not
a beginning nor an end
yet you persist
as though you were.

As I sit
I hear
it's not what I see
it's a blur for me
the sound of my heart
to forgive.

Nature in soul
I hear your call to me it
has reached the depth
of the meaning of life to be
If only I can reach the sound of you're heart
beating through the voice
of your chirp in the music of nature
That you bring to me
I hear now that I am alive with you
Your call goes not unheard.

My inner voice unheard
why do I avoid thee
I shun your sound from my ears
To hear not your call
For what reason do I desire old age
to die away from this world.

The mountains are high
and I stand at its peak
seeing all what is below me the
sacrifices of myself and others
so I can stand tall.

Life is a healing dynamic
that can bring you out of the gloom
and doom of existence
let it
don't hold yourself back

Sometimes we cannot forgive
our own transgressions
and inflict pain against our soul body and mind
to never recover what is lost.

Source of hope
love to cope
and wisdom to share
one who cares with
golden hair
always near to remove the fear.

Oh my earth
you call to me
to see the truth of the word
and blossom a new day of love and hope for life.

Let your journey
be one of truth
and don't let the lies
of what you are not
cloud your vision of future realities.

Where I am
you are to be
and in that moment
we see that we are the same reality
not in time or of mind
just a spiritual being.

Life has for you
a special gift to open
but you need to put your hands
on the wrapping
in all its colors and beauty.

We must move past
the barrier of time in space
and reach to the unknown truth
that we are a spirit
guided by our own insight.

We become the ideal
by ideally becoming that
which we desire to be.

Darkness of life
a lie within
that I——you——
cannot win.

When we approach something
that is a truth
we first may cry
get angry
or go into apathy
Experience it and truth will prevail.

The world
cannot survive the evil of a few
while the majority turn away
and don't act
to help their fellow man.

We are now in the eternity
of who we are
and not kept from realizing the freedom before us.
We must take responsibility for it.

If we are to find peace
we must first find truth
in the goodness of others
that they too are able to find peace within.

Never allow
another to limit you
in how you can be in the potential you can become
and be in the strength of your own soul.

I need not justify my right
to know all knowledge
that I am able to obtain from any source.
The right to certainty is for all.

I am the enlightened
being of my own soul
the truth of my own insight
into all realities subjective
and objective.

Without meaning
there can be no understanding
and that meaning is within you
but you have to find it
and you can.

In the spirit of man
lies all that is best in who he is
We can now bring man
to the awareness of his spiritual self.

If you find you need me
in your moment of pain
say my name
and I shall appear in that place where life has no shame.

While I sit in life's room
of quiet moments
I hear its voice of reason
to carry me through.

In the life you live
be then the person you are
and deny not
your beauty within.

If I see not the shadow
of my own blindness in life
and fail to move to the light
of my own way
how am I to find truth?

Follow the purpose
of the material universe
and become it as mass
in the chaos
of your own destruction.

Some will kill your purpose
and desire to bury it
before you have a chance
to live it out in life.

Who you are
must be defined by your purpose
to be alive or you fail.

A purpose denied in life
without any reason to exist continuing life's destiny
of emptiness to persist.

Confidence in the value
of oneself to produce an effect
that will be received favorably
will determine if you will be successful.

The purpose behind
what is to be produced
is senior in importance
when determining the value of it.

If you value your communication
and it is valued by another
you have the basis
by which you can become rich—
Communicate.

The value of exchange
is the basis of all communication
determined by acknowledging
your concept of self-worth.

I am as I am
and not how I am to be
to be then as I am.

When your life has become not
what your heart beats for then
you are dead
and will not be alive
until you beat to a different drum.

Some may say the future
is an unforeseen
that is not within our grasp.
You are the future
own it
and become in it your truth.

Becoming other
than who you are
is only a difference of potential to have
more or less.
You choose which one.

It is easy to deny
that we are not to become anything
other than who we are
but for that to be true
we must see the future.

The meaning of existence
is to bring the spiritual
into a physical form
as the outward manifestation
of who we are to become.

How are you to conquer anything
if you are unwilling
to confront your challenge
to overcome the obstacles
to finally win?

It is not what has been
that determines our success
it's what we will into existence
in the moment
for there to be a future.

We all see
what we want to view
not what in reality is
or should be
and fail to live in truth
our own integrity.

All upsets occur with a failure
and an unwillingness to view
the lie that perpetrates itself
underlying all conflicts.

We seek to understand
without being understood
and find ourselves lost in our journey
to be aware of who we are.

If you're feeling like you're going nowhere
to be somewhere
and the somewhere is not anywhere
discover the true you.

When you don't know
where you come from
where you are or going to.
Become all three
to be none of them anywhere
and you will be free.

If you are sitting in a void
of understanding
and have not the insight
into the meaning of your own existence
Fill the void by being it.

Without a purpose to attain wisdom
and the necessity
to have it to survive
There is no useful reason to obtain it.

Knowledge to be had
must be desired and reached for
to have a value to you
what that knowledge can bring.

The single most valuable thing in life
is knowledge.

A plan cannot be fulfilled
unless it has a purpose
driving it through
to overcome all stops.

He who walks alone
will find himself without a direction
to lead or follow anyone
anywhere in life.

The vision of tomorrow is
within the perspective of
how you see
where you are going from where you are.

Happy am I
that I am the life I live
to be the life I give
to myself and others.

How are we to know
if we assume without inspection
the facts of the unknown
believed to be true.

You have decided not to know
and knowing that you don't
will leave you enslaved
by your ignorance within.

The mind is the mirror
of what we imagine can be
or what has been.

We are as we agree and
reality is only what is
because you caused it to be.

My life is worthy of you
only if the value of me
gives truth of who we are
to be for each other.
In that regard we are friends.

He who whispers lies
brings chaos to those who hear
and fear abounds
where violence is found.

Why be an enslaver being
To then be one
in your own trap of pain
for having wronged another.

I deny not
the I of my soul
and bring to the living the gift of life.

In the presence of greatness
we rise to be better than who we are.
Be great and help others rise too.

I seek not to be
that which I am
and become not
what I am to be,

me.

If you don't try to understand
how can anything be understood
to learn how to make life good?

If you could bring
the meaning of life
to someone who would it be and what would life mean?

Where is the darkness
of what cannot be known
and who will shine light
in a needy mind?

As I weep
through the days of forgotten souls
whose life could not be
I hear not the cry of birth

given to me.

I am as I am
not because of what I have been
but because of who I am to be.

I seek not
the power over others
but instead give direction
for you to have power
over yourself.

He who would bring
the word that is within
has given of themselves
for the salvation of others.

A child steps through
the poverty of life
to suffer for the want of love.

Whisper the sound of your voice
and bring me into a place of love
that only you can give
so I can live.

Is now not the time
to enter upon what is our future destiny
in the moment of creation?

Our eyes of future realities
see not the scene of how it should be
and become denied
in its freedoms of hope faith and charity.

As we seek truth
are we
to be the truth that we see?

My Mother Earth
your heartbeat and life's force tortured by
our failure to feel the body of your soul
that we destroy.

Find the courage to change
and bring yourself to take responsibility
for the condition you find yourself in
and be free.

The mind of evil
cannot look at the good
they have lost
because they cannot forgive
their actions of destruction.

The rational of one
may be rejected by the many
even though the one is doing
what is in the greater good
of Mankind.

Trust not the words of a person
but the actions that represent truth
of what was is and should be
in the context of reason.

The concept is the idea
behind all originality
and is the basis by which all life has been created.

Living
is being the author
of your own life.

When life has a gift
use it
and you will find the joy
of being you.

Please know
that what I write
is not a state of mind I am
in——it is a poetic statement of reality.

I am now

as you see me

and I you

and we are blind

of who we are

for there to be a way

to see again as beings.

My inner being awaits
to be liberated from the oppressed state
I am in
to be the origin of truth
and all of what I could become.

My love of wisdom
is my soul's delight
and why I write.

The master awaits and
you find not the truth
he seeks for you
to be free
from your own demise.

A mind of thought
fraught by ignorance of reason
to be at war
over failed concepts of truth to
never become what is right.

Oh time
you take me from nowhere
to be somewhere
that is not anywhere
In this illusion of infinite foreverness
of nothingness.

He who will not find truth
in all what should be
will be buried in the torture of lies
fueled by the hatred of freedom.

People of the earth
gather now
for the time is come
to be no more as you are
to be as I am
the moment in creation
of all what is.

I am in
while I am out
to be out of what I am in
I am as I am
of what I am to be in for
where I am.

Is the answer
to the unknown
the known answer to
the knowing answer
of what is known.

We must find within
what has always been our ability
to know and find truth.

The value of you
is measured by the worth
you are in service to others.

A man can only lose
what he has not acquired
by neglecting who he is to himself
to admire.

We sit idle watching
the seconds go by
and time has no meaning
only that it ticks away our
delay in doing what is our
salvation.

A man serves not the soul
and grows old
to find himself lifeless
with no one to be his friend
not even himself.

All efforts to acquire
in the physical universe
the physical universe will be for nothing
if it does not advance your spirituality.

Never work to remain the same
in what we build for it
will leave you without.

We are as we are
to be not how we have been
to improve.
We can know about what we don't.

Silence me
and I become a voice of reason
to sound the alarms
of those who would suppress mankind's right
to know truth.

Silent I am
shunned for speaking truth
to pierce the enemy's heart of lies
who are destroying life.

Silence my voice unheard
how can I be the voice of my own soul and who will listen?

A child betrayed
wonders alone
locked away
in a prison grave of abuse drug strangling their soul a truth untold.

In living do we reach to know each other
in the oneness of creation
or do we see ourselves as different
rejecting God's view of Mankind?

My love
cannot be measured in time
nor can it be lived
fully in one life.

I am as I believe myself to be and in the reality of forgotten souls
trapped to a planet of men who see not the truth
of how to be free.

So many are concerned about success
and failed to see
that they only need to be their best

and life will take care of the rest.

How to succeed at losing
will teach you the wisdom
on how to win at winning
this introduced the game of life.

If you see not the way within
then you do not know
from where you became
and that is why you remain
an unknown being to you.

I am not
at the end of my life I
am at the beginning
of whatever will end
that was the beginning
of whatever will be.

Smile if you are not happy
and the smile will outwit
what you are unhappy about.

Are we the beginning of what is
and are we the end of what will be
then why do we worry
about the details of anything?

Don't be afraid
of what could become
but embrace the reason
you are alive
to discover the unknown.

On high we stand
for the integrity of who we are
and become the best we can be
to learn of the way
we once were.

To succeed start digging and the well of prosperity
will present itself for you to engage in and your future will be assured
as you dream it to be.

In the ocean of freedom
I rise to the winds of the storm in my life to fight not
but to embrace it with courage and strength.

Love as I am
to become who I am to be and then I will be free.

Deny not the love you desire and belong to those
who bring true happiness.

Love needs to live
but love must be able to give
of itself to live.

My love
my desire is to be the admiration of your day
only because I please you in every way.

Caught in the world of the unknown
and unable to see
I wait
and no voice I hear to guide me through.

Bring into the world
of what is unreal
to discover the truth of what is.

I bring you me
and do care that I am here
and you there to love
and give life a reason to live.

We are to journey
through the poverty of the forgotten
with the integrity to help
and do right by all in need.

Looking through the eyes of color
I see not the soul within
and fail to love
what is beautiful.

I stand to bring
what has not been
to see it through to the end.

Give me the truth as it is to be
and let that truth go into the world
and bring freedom to all those
who will listen to its call.

Am I one with you
or do I deny who that may be
undefined and without the meaning
of this living soul that I have
become?

I hear your heartbeat of life
and with each one
I feel your living soul within me
and I am blessed to be one with you.

Burning light of reason
our thoughts now true
we stand and wait no more for
you have arrived to deliver us.

Burning flame
spirit soul we see you
your love burns
we bow to your greatness we are now in eternity.

The flame of source it burns the remorse
of all that is undesired to replace it with what is admired.

As we view
who we are in the mirror
of our own soul
are we what the view is
or is this the lie of illusion.

You are the eye of your own truth.

Am I the word of thought
to be not the symbol of what I am

a man.

My vision unseen
to see what is the view what is not
in the reality of illusion.

As we reach the unknown
uncertainty of certainty
blindness bends the mind
toward ignorance of bliss.

Through the graveyard of yesterday we have today a tomorrow
one without sorrow
if we shed not the blood of evil.

A man lives not
by the wealth of his ways
but by the spirit of his goodness at heart
bestowed upon him
by the grace of the Lord.

The idea is the reason
beyond all what is
so if you are not comfortable
with the reality you are in change your ideas about it.

Our shameful past
need not stay lay them now
to heaven's grave for
forgiveness abounds.

Women who protect
never neglect
for they are freedom to lose or win for all men.

Women cause life to be
then why are they in life
not free?

Men the pain we cause
is in return to learn for
what not to do
unless we die and feel no shame
how our actions cause such pain.

A child waits for a voice
unheard. Who will hear their
deepest fear? The touch of life
innocence lost save the child at
any cost.

A woman receives the life
of sorrow and shame so
we can live through this
evil/good game.

A child cries
the voice of pain
when those that kill
are so insane.

A woman's voice unheard
from a soul in torment
in quiet places
where silence destroys.

Are you the idea
or is the idea a by-product of your intent
if the idea is not you
then who is the cause of the idea
the spirit?

We all want to understand
to be understood
but to understand on how to be understood
we must look at how others understand.

I cannot exist within any reality
that I have not had a prior decision to be there
so I cannot truly be a victim
of anything or anyone.

What I consider will be is
and only if I consider it
otherwise it will not be real
and have no power over
me or my existence.

Only you can determine
if what you believe in is true
according to your own observation and there is no other truth.

All life is in the spirit
creating it to be
a place to live
in form
and to create a place
for truth to be revealed.

The message of life is
that we are to live it
for it to be the life
of the message.

All that we have
is this moment and the next
to lead to the next
but what will they amount to
if we don't love?

Someone near needs you
who are they
Care enough to know
find what their needs are and help.

Don't feel alone
when you are at your worst
those who love you will be near
if you ask them too
it's okay to need.

When life seems over
there is nowhere to hide
and all what you desire has left inside
Know I love you
pass it on.

I deny myself
and what I can accomplish
and keep my soul
from the freedom to be,
I am in treason to me.

If I am to be today
not as yesterday
I must leave behind my longing
to be left alone.

Life today
is a struggle to belong
disconnect
or create one's own reality.

When others deny who you are
become more present
until they retreat.

In all of us
is the will to survive
and what kills that will
is the denial of self.

When you see not
the beauty in each of us
the darkness will destroy who we are
and who we are to become.

It's better to cry
in attempts to win at something
then to lose
by not trying at all.

Have you given
to those forgotten
on this day
when sad hearts
have no one to say
I love you?

Today we bring
our hearts together
with the same life force that sustains us.

My love for you
on this day is without meaning or explanation
it comes with no condition
or need to be acknowledged.

Love is what your gift
can be to another
it does not need wrapping or fancy paper
just heart, soul and integrity.

We are humanity a
species of creation
of all what is best in all of us
but fail to regard the gift
and the beauty of reason.

I am of you
as you are of me
to have without
slavery what is
mutual giving.

Have no fear
for fear has no strength
in the understanding of what was
is or will be.

A way to know
is in the understanding of how but
the how is in the word of the how
to be understood.

Speak to the truth of who you are as I am
and we can have the reality of oneness
that is our destiny.

A time to see what isn't
to experience what is
to become what is not
and never has been.

If I fail to see my journey as one
then will I stray
only to be lost in time?

How can I become the truth that I am
in the lies that I am not believed to be
that I am
what have I become?

Only you can know you
to know who is the one
that will save you.

Am I not the one of oneness
that is the isness of all reality
to be the reality of oneness of all?

I have given you life
so life can bring you to me
in the unknown of what was
but could never become.

If you are not the way
then where are you
in your eternal understanding
of your salvation of self?

I am here
to be the awareness
for you to know truth.

Your journey to me is my way to you
for you to find that I am
the I am
of the cause of existence.

I am the creation
of all that is
and will be the way
to the truth of my word
for you to know me.

I seek only to be heard in
the whisper of my voice
in quite unassuming moments
that bring us together.

I have been here
without being and
now that I am
where am I
How can I exist in the unknown reality
of my existence?

My child taken from my creation
to be without the love of whom I
am in them to bring to the world
the word I speak.

I want what I don't see
and see what I don't want
and have in mind what cannot be and become what I am not—
how can I change?

Let's take the time
to see how life is a journey
to the next moment of experience that will give us what we need
to make it to the next.

If you are always trying to be your best
without understanding
how you became your worst you will never learn to be at rest?

When you feel
you cannot go on
it only means
that you must remain to learn too.

I love your smile
the warmth of your touch
the words you speak
it brings me to you in the way I seek.

Know our love
and we become the oneness
we desire in a world
where belonging is everything we require.

As I love you
the presence of your soul astounds me
in the beauty of who you are
and there I remain.

Take my love in
be for me as I am to be for myself
in the want of
and need for acceptance.

A soldier's tears fall silent
in the graveyard of the battlefield
while the breath of his comrade
leaves him forever.

A soldier sits
he hears not the sound of peace
that we enjoy
and is burdened with the assault
to it by enemies of good.

What you know of what is
is not what you will know
of what can be
so never live in the past understanding
of anything.

Be guided
not into a false sense of security
through believing knowledge is limited
to what is already known.

The failure of cutting communication
is refusing life the right to live
and in so doing you prevent
the rewards it gives.

To make others wrong
is to destroy their heart within
causing pain that should never begin.

The discovery of truth
does not mean we should make others wrong
but only to teach them what is right.

Honesty can lead to
what is not true
to discover what is, so
be willing to forgive.

Live life
and give all
what is a chance to arrive
for in that giving of self
others have a chance to become?

As we sit
and ponder over life
living may pass us by
where the answer is
and why.

What you observe is truth
not what someone else says it is
without inspection.
Know thyself and you are free.

I long to be heard
and not ignored
for the good I bring and
yet the music I sing has
no one to hear it
for in the melody is truth.

How can I become
that which I am
if I am
to become again.

Crushed into a mass meaning
of yesterday's pain
of all life's weary moments
of why we came
to discover not
but to wrought from being
anything imagined.

I am forever in the sky
and where I go
I don't know why
and when I get there I will see and
then when the sun goes down I
will be with me.

Weathering away
why stay
to play without joy
a game
that will only destroy?

How can I become
that which I am
if I am
to become again?

Visit the unknown
shown only if I view not
what is only then
will I live.

Mother!

We became one, as a son, to be, to see, each other. Brothers and Sisters, too, you gave.

We are because you were to give life for us to live. We stand now, in our humble way, to say we love you.

You forgave our falls and called us your own, to be for us, to get through our troubled ways. For that we say thank you.

Filled at times, of our own concern, to learn of what not to do, to have our own lives, to find our own truth.

We now share because you care that we are one. In this creation different, yet the same in spirit of one truth.

We cried, we laughed, and went our different ways, but will be in a place the same.

Mother, you walked with little to say, but when you spoke, love came to tell me of how we should be.

In this sea of troubled souls, when will we be in that presence of whom you really are, a mother who has come far, to reach for her children in need, a mother true to her calling, to see it through to the end, which only means we will begin again, new in spirit and form, to mourn not of yesterday, but to play as angels do, because we did it right and made it through.

What justice will come when we leave this place that we came to visit, for a journey of learning to pass us by, to be in that place where angels fly.

I will see you then and I wish you well.

Until then, now, I will bid you farewell.

A Mother's Gift!

A mother's gift is her love divine. It passes through our troubled mind. In our thoughts we fail to view, who a mother is until she is through.

A mother's thought is one of joy, for her children, girls and boys.

A mother's wish is that we do our best, so that in life we pass the test.

A mother's prayer is that we turn out right, to be and do our best. Before she can truly be at rest.

A mother's will is to fill a void that a child needs to have peace and joy.

A mother's tears are pain we don't see, so we can live our lifetime without evil deeds.

A mother's desire is that her children forgive, to let the lies pass so our heart can live.

A mother knows the past is gone, why then should her children make each other wrong?

A mother hears all what is said, but does it matter to those we love if we end up dead.

A mother's life she gives to lend a hand, to love and serve a gift to man.

A mother's life is alone to mourn and cry, when we can't see, how in her heart, try's, to fulfill our deepest needs.

A mother wakes when the baby cries. While we sleep, she wipes the tears from their eyes.

A mother's song is music to the soul, for the young and for the old.

A mother writes in words a truth, giving us guidance, so we make it through.

A mother gives birth in so much pain, but is filled with joy and glad we came.

A mother waits while her children tell their story, that they have wronged her and for that they are sorry.

A mother's gift is her love divine to keep, and when she gone, this we will learn when we weep.

A mother whispers lovingly that we are special indeed, because of who we are, she always sees.

A mother wants nothing in return, but gives it her all, for her children to learn.

A mother holds a child to comfort its soul, always in life no matter how old.

A mother knows when we are weak, sees into our heart when we sleep.

A mother tries even if she may fail, to give us courage for her children to tell a different tale.

A mother stands always strong, in a gentle form for us to belong, to each other in every way. Love your Brothers and sisters now and when after I am laid to the grave.

A mother knows the road will be rough, but deep down she teaches her children to be tough.

A mother cares when no one will, it keeps us quiet and our souls still.

A mother waits for no one to decide, if she will love or let love pass her by.

Thoughtful Regard

May we bring our hearts divine,
to all who come with trouble minds.

May we seek to find in each other,
that we truly are, a sister and a brother of mankind.

May we lift up in how we instruct,
and not to offend with our conduct.

May we give and not take and fail to relate,
to a needy soul before it is too late.

May we look for good in all that we do,
not to find fault to suit me and you.

May we bless those in need that suffer alone,
with no place, they can call home.

May we move together to bring peace,
not to steal and, through others, cheat.

May we calm a storm of a troubled soul,
in the young and the old.

May we gather in trust,
so that we are all doing what we know we must.

May we never neglect to try to understand,
that we are one with our fellow man.

May we journey through a path of light,
to forgive and forget what was not right.

May we say what we mean in love and truth,
so those who hear us are blessed by what we say and do.

May we come to understand that all truths may not be the same,
but we must learn them, at times, just the same.

May we not hide behind lies and fear,
but hold to our hearts that to God all are dear.

May we sit in quiet times,
listening to the call of angels to free man's minds.

You're never alone to ride the waves,
to weather the storm,
and calm the day.

Patrick Walsh